FRED TRUEMAN'S
Dales Journey

FRED TRUEMAN'S
Dales Journey

Left. I've always been struck by the flat, wide nature of Wensleydale's floor, particularly when compared to many of the other Yorkshire dales. The valley's character is plainly seen in this view looking out from one of the windows of Bolton Castle. The high ground to the right is Penhill, towering above the straggling village of West Witton.

First published in Great Britain 1998 by
Dalesman Publishing Company Limited
Stable Courtyard
Broughton Hall
Skipton
North Yorkshire BD23 3AZ
Published in paperback 2000
Text © Fred Trueman
Photographs © Simon Warner, Colin Raw, John Morrison, Keith Watson,
David Coates, Richard Cochrane

A British Library Cataloguing in Publication record is available for
this book

ISBN 1 85568 188 9

Designed by Jonathan Newdick
Typeset by SPAN Graphics Limited
Colour Origination by Grasmere (Digital Imaging) Limited
Printed by Midas Printing (HK) Limited

Photographic acknowledgements

Dave Coates 37 (top), 45, 48 (left, top
right, bottom right), 49, 54, (bottom),
68, 69 (bottom), 77

Richard Cochrane 37 (bottom), 69
(top), 76, 79 (bottom)

John Morrison 10 (left and right), 20,
21, 46, 47, 71, 78, 79 (top), 85, 90
(top), 98 (top), 103, 107, 111 (top),
112, 113, 116 (top)

Colin Raw 9, 15 (right), 22, 27 (top),
27 (bottom), 28, 29, 30, 31, 38, 39, 51,
54 (top), 58, 59, 108, 109, 110, 111
(bottom), 114, 115, 117, 118, 119, 125,
128, 129, 130, 131, 132, 133, 135,
136–7, 138, 139, 140, 141, 142, 143

Simon Warner 2, 6, 12, 13, 15 (left),
16, 18, 19, 24–5, 26, 32, 33 (bottom),
35, 36, 40, 43, 50, 52, 53, 55, 56–7, 60,
63, 64, 74, 75, 80, 87, 88–9, 92, 93 (top
and bottom), 95, 96, 97, 100, 104–5,
116 (bottom), 120–1, 122, 126, 134

Keith Watson 17, 23, 33 (top), 34, 65,
67, 70, 72–3, 83, 86, 90 (bottom), 91,
94 (top and bottom), 98 (bottom), 99

Contents

Introduction

I love and adore the drive up Sleddale, following the course of Gayle Beck, away from Hawes and up and over into Langstrothdale. The road climbs steeply and offers some superb views. Sleddale has a scattering of farms and the one in this picture looks most appealing with a foreground of bright buttercups.

It was cricket, appropriately enough, which led to me discovering the glories of the Dales. Way back in 1960, in the days when I was fighting fit and bowling fast, I found myself in the Yorkshire side playing a pre-season practice match on a Saturday afternoon at the picturesque Settle ground. At the time, I'd never been to the Dales and I didn't even know where Settle was. I drove over from Scarborough by way of Otley and Ilkley and on through Skipton, eventually picking a route along the road to Settle. It was a journey which was to change my life.

As I crested the tops and began to drop down into Skipton, I was amazed to see the surrounding hills. This was an entirely different Yorkshire to the one I knew. I was born in the mining hamlet of Stainton in South Yorkshire and, up to then, lived out on the coast of North Yorkshire. Enjoying a welcome pint after the cricket, I commented on the beauty of the countryside and was told: "You haven't seen anything yet." My hosts advised me to head back via Grassington and Gargrave. On the way, I went past what is now the drive of my home, never thinking that one day I would end up living there.

From that day, I was spellbound by the Dales. And I returned, year after year, as something I can't really put my finger on kept drawing me back to this enticing part of the world. I don't know exactly what it was, but to me the Dales were fascinating. And, in 1969, I got to the point where I said to myself that the Dales were where I wanted to live. With my new wife, Veronica, I started looking for a suitable spot and found it in a secluded cottage near a pleasant beck five miles from the Wharfe and a couple of miles from the Aire. Here was peace, privacy and nature in abundance. It was the start of a great adventure – of exploring the Dales, of getting to know their people, of feeling truly at home. It was one of the greatest moves of my life.

Catrigg Force, high above Stainforth to the east of the village, makes a spectacular burst of water on Stainforth Beck after heavy rain. It is generally regarded that they are the finest falls in the Craven district as they take a double leap into a lovely rocky plunge adorned with mature trees.

I've always been a countryman. I can't stand towns, I hate them. I was born and bred in the country, though the sights and sounds of industry were never far away in Stainton. Our hamlet consisted of 12 colliers' houses and although you couldn't see the pit, hidden down in the valley bottom, you knew it was there. A railway line ran a quarter of a mile from our house and steam engines clanked and roared along it day and night. There was a stream at the bottom of the school field and it was a peaceful spot – but nothing like the great rivers of the Dales. The nearest river to me as a child was probably the Don, and that was badly polluted by the industries in Sheffield. It was a quiet spot, but not as special as the place in the Dales where I now live. It's idyllic here and I love and adore it – and I always will.

I usually refer to the Dales as 'God's Country' and I can sit in the countryside here for an hour, smoking my pipe, thinking how beautiful it is. I feel I'm a very, very lucky man to have been able to play cricket like I did, to have travelled the world like I did, but still to be able to come back to the Dales. I don't want to go anywhere else. The Dales are like different people, each with different personalities and different moods. There's always something to watch and enjoy in the Dales. But although I've got the good fortune to live in the country, I'm only three hours by train from the centre of London. I'm even lucky in that.

When I am returning to the Dales after one of my regular trips to distant parts of the country, if I'm in the car, when I get within eight or nine miles of home I can see the top of Sharp Haw, which rises to more than a thousand feet. It gets bigger and bigger as I get closer to it. It's a great feeling. It shows, in the time I've been here, the strength of the bond that has developed between myself and the Dales.

When you come and live in the Dales, you get into a different way of life. It's a slower way of life, make no mistake about it. For example, I travel all around the Dales and I can see more sets of traffic lights in one street in Leeds than I can in the whole of the Dales.

When I'm in places like London, people talk about Yorkshire and I say to them: "Have you ever seen Yorkshire?" They say: "I've been to Leeds and Sheffield." And I say: "No, have you seen Yorkshire?" Of course, there has to be an industrialised part of the county and we have that, though it's not like it used to be. But one of my pet sayings is that when

There's a lovely place by the road near Gunnerside where I like to stand and look out across Swaledale and enjoy the sight of its walls and barns. This view captures both in a fascinating way.

The valley-side looms out of the murk in this interesting view of the landscape between Muker and Keld.

I get up in a morning, my birds are singing, not coughing. Some people look at me and I don't think they know what I mean. But a lot of others I've met who have visited the Dales tell me how beautiful they are and tell me what a lucky man I am to live there.

I meet people from all over the country who have the same feelings about the Dales as I do. They don't know what it is, but they are fascinated by the Dales and want to live there. I've met Australians, New Zealanders and South Africans who have said to me: "I've heard you talk about the Dales, Freddie, and you're right – aren't they beautiful?"

One of the most remarkable things about the Dales is the weather. You can get four seasons all in one day. I've seen sunshine, rain and snow on the same day. It's nice to look out of my lounge window in winter and see Sharp Haw and if there is snow on the tops, you'd think you were in Switzerland. I've had friends to stay and they ask why, when we have all this on our doorstep, we would want to go away on holiday. It's true.

Spring is my favourite time of year in the Dales. I love seeing the countryside coming to life, when all the daffodils, tulips and narcissuses are coming out and you've got a lovely, sunny day. But it can get cold here and I love to have a log fire blazing in the grate. In the winter, with the curtains closed and the logs burning, it's absolutely superb. It's especially nice if I can get hold of some apple logs – if Veronica has lit a fire, they are lovely to smell when I come in through the gate.

I'm also very interested in birds – I love to watch them. I'm very fortunate in that there are more than 130 species within a mile's radius of my garden. We have owls in the woodland round about and sometimes on warm, sunny evenings, I like to sit in the garden and listen to them.

One problem I have in my garden is caused by a sparrowhawk. He seems to think it's a takeaway. I have some lovely coal tits, great tits, long-tailed tits and blue tits, but the sparrowhawk keeps turning up and messing them around.

I do get fed up of people coming out of towns to live in the country and complaining about country life. They moan about the cockerel crowing at five in the morning. What do they expect the cockerel to do? He's done it for a million years. Then they complain about the foul smell when farmers are manuring their fields, which they have to do. It's something you get used to and something you never notice. I've had

The top end of Swaledale is pretty rugged. This view is looking downdale from near to the village of Thwaite. Richard Kearton, a pioneering wildlife photographer, was born here and a cottage bears his initials and carvings of birds and beasts on its front door surround.

people stay with me who say they can't sleep because it's too quiet. Others say they had a lovely night's sleep until the birds began the dawn chorus. I never hear it now, or the cockerel crowing, because I've got so used to it. I get in my car and if the farmers have been manuring their fields it doesn't bother me. It's all part of country life and if you want to live in the country, you have to abide by everything that goes on there.

People living in concrete jungles complain about foxes being killed in the Dales. But they've no idea what it's about. I love foxes, I think they're beautiful creatures, but I've seen what damage they can do to farms. And on more than one occasion, I've stopped my car when I've seen visitors taking the top stones off dry-stone walls. They say they're just taking one or two home for their rockery. But if everybody does that, there'd be no dry-stone walls left. Those of us who are fortunate enough to live in the Dales try to keep them tidy and care for them.

A lot of people may think Dalesfolk are odd, but once you get to know them you realise they aren't at all. You soon discover what great people they are. They look at strangers as strangers until they get to know them. I've had some wonderfully happy hours in the Dales. I used to go to a pub in one of the neighbouring villages and got to know all the locals. Even though I was what I suppose you could call a personality, they never bothered me and always looked after me.

Driving over the passes between the dales is just as enjoyable as driving down the valleys themselves. Buttertubs is one of my favourite passes – up there, I feel as though I'm on top of the world. This is the view looking down into Wensleydale.

Dalesfolk don't mind playing jokes. A pub called The Angel at Hetton, near Grassington, used to get pretty full in the summer, but there were always two seats in front of the window and the Dales people very rarely touched them. A couple of strangers would come in and sit in them and the locals in the pub would watch and await developments. The landlord had a spaniel called Duke. In the summer, the moths would get in the window and the dog used to go after them, straight over the table, sending beer and glasses flying everywhere. The visitors would be drenched and we'd all fall about laughing. It always got a laugh.

I remember late one night after official closing time when Cracoe, the local village cricket team, had won the Dales Cup and they were all in the pub celebrating. I looked in to see what was happening. There was the gamekeeper in there, farmers, a poacher, the squire, the blacksmith, myself and the landlord. Eventually, the copper turned up and joined in as well. It was like a piece of Olde England all in that one little place. It really took you back in time to see it.

I love telling Yorkshire stories and one of my favourites is from the Dales: a bloke came up from the south of England to stay at Grassington and he'd heard about Dales people getting up very early. He set his alarm and was walking down the road about half past four in the morning when he saw a farmer, carrying a pail of milk, coming towards him.

"Lovely morning," said the visitor. The farmer replied: "Aye, it was early on."

I remember once doing some filming for a local television company with some horses at Kilnsey in Wharfedale. We used the village green and a very irate woman gave us a rollicking for messing it up. Whether we had or not, I don't know. There might have been a bit of jealousy because she wasn't part of the filming. People in the Dales villages, though warm and friendly, can be very parochial.

There's tremendous cricket in the Dales. After I'd retired from the first class game, Cracoe persuaded me to play for them in the evening Dales League. I gave them my big, old leather cricket bag which had been round the world with me, and one or two other things, to help them. I played for them, and I have an affinity for them. I still see the lads and help them out if I can. It was great fun playing in the Dales.

Many great cricketers used to love visiting and talking about the Dales, which have had a strong connection with Yorkshire players. Herbert Sutcliffe, the Yorkshire and England opening batsman, and Hedley Verity, the Yorkshire and England slow left-arm bowler, were big fans of the Dales. I remember one occasion when my then bank manager took me to lunch at The Old Hall in Threshfield. I was leaning on the bar in the corner talking when some old boy said to me: "It reminds me, Freddie, of Hedley Verity seeing you standing there. He used to put his elbow exactly where you've got yours now."

Great cricketers such as Ray Lindwall, Don Bradman and Jack Fingleton tell me that they still think of the Dales. Neil Hawke, whom I dismissed for my 300th wicket in Test cricket, lived near Nelson in Lancashire for a while and spent a bit of time in the Dales. And my mate Peter Parfitt, who hails from Norfolk, thinks the Dales are absolutely marvellous and now lives at Elslack, just down the road from Skipton. The Australian Press boys also loved the Dales. They used to stay in the Devonshire Arms at Bolton Abbey, rather than be based in Leeds.

Outside cricket, rugby is my favourite game. I love both codes and the Wharfedale rugby union club, which plays at Threshfield, is tremendous. They've done a great job up there. It's a lovely little ground in a wonderful setting, they have floodlights and lots of teams, with kids as young as nine playing.

The green-domed chapel of Giggleswick School was, before its renovation, a well-known landmark in the Settle area. The surrounding hills, flecked with limestone outcrops, make a pleasing backdrop and hint of the scenic joys to come when you venture further up the dale.

How to make industry look beautiful! This is the Dewhirst Mill chimney on the Leeds to Liverpool Canal at Skipton. The photographer had to set his alarm early, for this is sunrise, not sunset.

Here's how to do a hard day's work!
The care and precision needed to build
a solid dry-stone wall is obvious in this
view of a waller in Wharfedale. Wallers
seem to be very much a dying breed,
but it's a craft which must be
encouraged to survive for future
generations to learn and enjoy.

There's a lot of history and tradition in the Dales. You still see farmers
building dry-stone walls, even though it seems to be a dying art. I was
up in Aysgarth in Wensleydale recently and watched a fellow called
Colin Simpson making hay rakes. He gave me one and I still have it in
the house.

There's a lot of wonderful food to be found in the Dales. You can still
pick up Wensleydale cheeses with different flavours, fine pickles and
you can still find home-fed cured ham. These are the proper cured hams,
not like the brine cured ones which are dipped into a brine bath for 24
hours and then taken out. I've never had ham anywhere in the world like
a Yorkshire home-fed ham. It's a different taste to any other. When you
see a proper Yorkshire home-fed cured ham, you can see the mould and
crust on it. I used to go up to the White Lion at Cray in Wharfedale for

Leyburn stands at the heart of Wensleydale and is a busy place, particularly when the market is in full swing. The village, once outshone by neighbouring Wensley and Middleham, was developed in the 17th century by the man who was to become the Duke of Bolton to replace the failed market centre of Wensley. Its name is said to derive from 'le borne', meaning stream by a clearing.

one reason and one reason only – for Major Horner's home-fed ham and eggs, bread and butter and tea. It was out of this world.

A fresh trout out of the Wharfe is absolutely beautiful – no doubt about it. I'm not a fisherman, never have been, but I can sit by a river like the Wharfe watching the fish, wishing I could get one out. There's nothing nicer than a trout straight out of the river into a pan. Another of my favourite dishes is blackberry and apple pie. Veronica and I gather wild blackberries in the Dales and she does a blackberry and apple pie which is absolutely wonderful.

I'm not a Dalesman, I'm what they call an offcumd'en. I've only been living here for 30 years, so I'm not accepted as a Dalesman – and rightly so. But I love living here in all this natural beauty.

No matter where you are in the Dales, there's something different to see. Even after 30 years of living here, their magic is still unbelievable – and I still can't explain it. They have a power which keeps pulling me back when I'm away and I just thank God that He let me come and live here.

The Dales, in all their variety, have so much to offer and my life has been considerably enriched by living among them. The pretty villages, sweeping hills, sparkling rivers, marvellous characters and absorbing history are a constant delight. I wouldn't exchange living in this part of England for any other.

The Wharfe at this point, where there's a wide sweep of the river, is dominated by the graceful sweep of the ruined arch of Bolton Abbey's east window. The Abbey, once the home of a small group of Augustinian canons, suffered in Henry VIII's Dissolution of the 16th century. It's said that Richard Moon, the last prior, tried to save the abbey from dissolution by sending a £10 bribe to Thomas Cromwell, the king's lieutenant. This failed to save the abbey and the monks were driven out in January 1540. These days it's a grand spot for a picnic.

Linton is a lovely village and boasts several crossings of the Wharfe. There is a clapper bridge, packhorse bridge, modern road bridge, stepping stones and a ford. They indicate times when the village was more important than it is these days. Linton is on the eastern boundary of the Craven district and I always feel the atmosphere is more of Craven than of the more hilly upper dale.

There seem to be quite a few places in Ribblesdale where hardy trees have taken root in the gaps in pieces of limestone pavement. This one, at Winskill Stones near Settle, seems to be clinging on for dear life.

The Swale sweeps round in a big
meander at Downholme Bridge, near
Marske, and is shown to perfection in
this wonderful shot of a watery sun
over the water.

This could only be Swaledale! A carpet of daisies and a glorious sky set off perfectly the stone in this section of dry-stone wall and a well-kept field barn.

Muker on a summer's morning. The church visible over the village's rooftops succeeded a small, thatched chapel built in 1850 so that Muker could have a consecrated churchyard. Before that, anyone who died in the upper dale had to be carried 16 miles to Grinton for burial.

Pages 24, 25. There are some idyllic footpaths around Horton-in-Ribblesdale. This is a view those walking the Pennine Way will enjoy. Just look at those immaculate dry-stone walls and imagine how much work has gone into building and maintaining them over the years.

To my mind, Ribblehead Viaduct on the beautiful Settle to Carlisle railway is a piece of engineering unrivalled anywhere in England. I've travelled over its 24 arches many times, but I have never stood at this spot and actually seen a train passing over. What a sight a steam engine, complete with those lovely old Pullman carriages, must make as it rumbles through. The train really is the best way to see Ribblesdale. You get a grand view of the Three Peaks. In this view, the whale-like hump of Whernside rises behind the viaduct and is capped with snow. It's like a miniature Switzerland.

Wharfedale has many moods with the changing seasons. Here the partly-frozen river makes a wonderful spectacle underneath a low sun at Kettlewell.

The Aire isn't the only watercourse in Airedale. The Leeds to Liverpool Canal passes through the valley and the section between Keighley and Skipton is particularly nice. With overhanging trees, distant views and a quiet path, it makes a lovely place to walk. Narrow boats, used by holidaymakers these days, are a colourful addition to the scene, especially if they are as well turned out as this one.

There's more to the area around Conistone than vast chunks of limestone – as this picture shows. It's a lovely meadow in early summer and makes for a peaceful, pastoral scene.

Farnhill Wood is noted for its magnificent displays of bluebells in the early summer. It's a lovely place to enjoy a quiet stroll, with the call of birds and the rustle of the wind in the leaves overhead for company.

Glorious weather puts the limestone
outcrops at Attermire Scar, near Settle,
in the best possible light.

The country lanes of the Dales are the perfect way to explore the region's more remote places. This minor road out of Ribblesdale, over the tops and round the back of Penyghent, is a particular favourite of mine and provides a less familiar perspective of the mountain.

It's very pleasant to park in Malham, walk up the road and then take the footpath to the Cove. The path and sheer limestone walls of the Cove are visible in this lovely shot. The Cove really is one of my favourite places in the Dales. It's a wonder of nature and something people travel for miles to see. I'm very lucky that it's virtually on my doorstep, just a 15-minute drive from home. Anyone who thinks Yorkshire is all about chimney stacks and smoke should be taken to see the Cove.

Farming plays a big part in the life of Swaledale and here a tractor and muck spreader pass through Thwaite.

The traditional, age-old way of doing things is, I'm pleased to say, alive and well in the Dales. This is a woodyard in Wensley, the village from which the valley takes its name. Note how neatly stacked the finished fence posts are.

Left. Aysgarth Falls are one of my favourite places, not just in Wensleydale, but in the whole of the Dales. When the River Ure is running high, as in this wintry view, the falls make a magnificent sight. I always marvel at the power of the water as it forces a path over the rocks.

Langstrothdale, through which the infant Wharfe flows, is a remote and almost secretive place. It's wonderful to pause here and enjoy the river. This cottage has a wonderful location, peaceful and quiet.

It's not just the sights and sounds of Wensleydale that are so appealing. The smells can be quite nice, too! Just imagine the pungent aroma of this wild garlic in woods close to Leyburn.

The Dales are famous for, among many other things, their sheep. These Dales-bred ewes seem to be enjoying a hearty meal on the slopes of Ten End, in the upper part of Wensleydale.

There's a lovely little story which goes along with the Polly Peachum Tower, near Wensley. The third Duke of Bolton heard an opera singer, Lavinia Senton, on the stage in London, singing the lead role of Polly Peachum in Gay's *The Beggar's Opera*. He fell in love with her and brought her back to Wensleydale to make her his second wife. The Duke built the tower, which he referred to as a summer house, so his wife did not have to practice her singing in the house. Even from the tower, it was said her voice could be heard a mile away at Bolton Hall!

This isn't far from my home. Cows graze peacefully on Eshton Moor's pastures close to Newfield Hall. It's a pleasant scene, with the hills an enticing prospect on the skyline.

Ewes grazing peacefully in a tranquil
summer scene as the sun sets over
Bradley.

Wharfedale

Lead mining was once a major industry in the Dales and even though it has faded from the scene, remains of its presence survive. These are buildings from mining days on Greenhow Hill, high above Wharfedale. This is a wonderful place for walking, offering all the peace and quiet anyone could wish for.

Wharfedale is possibly the most talked-about dale of them all and, at the risk of upsetting one or two people, I have to say it's my favourite and certainly the most beautiful. It's difficult to put into words just how beautiful Wharfedale is. It's unbelievable.

On a dull day it seems to have a mood all its own. On such days, I can look across the dale and imagine Ashley Jackson, the Yorkshire painter, magically capturing that cloudy mood on his canvas. Many's the time I've sat by the river and watched its changing moods. To me, Wharfedale has everything – hills, waters, valleys, lovely little villages, wonderful walks and a tremendous sense of history.

I've spent much of my time with the Wharfe. I go to church most Sundays at Bolton Priory which is on the Wharfe, and I play golf at Ilkley Golf Club which is on the Wharfe. I've ventured right the way up the dale to find the river's source and love and adore it up there. I've spent a lot of time in Kettlewell with friends and have had a lot of fun there, particularly in the Racehorses Hotel which is right on the Wharfe.

The Wharfe must be one of the cleanest rivers in England because there's no industry on it or pollution in it. When there has been heavy rain in the hills up the dale, the river level rises quickly and I believe it can travel along at 40 miles per hour. If, like me, you have been lucky enough to have seen the surge of the water when there has been heavy rain, you can see the water coming. I know in books that were written one hundred years ago, the river was referred to as "the fast-flowing Wharfe". It's a beautiful river, though it certainly has its dangers and has claimed many lives, particularly at The Strid, near Bolton Abbey. Here the river is penned in by rocks and is just six feet wide.

I've been right up above Buckden to see where the Wharfe rises, out of the wilderness of Langstrothdale Chase and alongside the road over

Fleet Moss linking Wharfedale with Wensleydale. It's nice to sit up there, on the grassy banks by the river, and watch the trout swimming lazily by. It fascinates me the way the water rises, becomes a river and then flows for miles and miles out to the east, past Otley, Collingham, Wetherby and Tadcaster, before eventually, at Cawood, joining up with the waters of the Swale, Ure and Nidd to become part of the Ouse.

I love to go up beyond Buckden, climb over the tops and stand and look across the valley and down into Wensleydale. There are some lovely walks around Buckden and hikers seem to enjoy them in both winter and summer.

Kilnsey is one of my favourite places in Wharfedale – it's the sort of spot to send the pulse racing. Several times I've stood beneath the magnificent overhanging rock of Kilnsey Crag and then walked up to the top above the village and enjoyed the panoramic views which go on for miles. In the old days, there was a challenge at this spot for young men looking to show off their manly prowess to their lady friends. The idea was to throw pennies at the face of the Crag from the road running along its base. They say the Crag's a bit of an optical illusion – it looks as though you could put out your hand and touch it from the road, but it's a long way away. It's so far away from the road that you can't hit the rock. I've never heard of anybody hitting the Crag with a penny, but many used to try, and then the local kids would go and find the pennies.

Kilnsey is also the venue for the annual show of the Upper Wharfedale Agricultural Society. By all accounts, it's a wonderful day out, with everything from dry-stone walling to harness racing.

There's a fine vantage point just down the road from Kilnsey, looking across the Wharfe towards Conistone. What a beautiful stretch of the river that is. When I look down at it in the middle of winter, with snow on the ground, I always think what a wonderful Christmas card the scene would make.

Across the river here is Grass Wood, where there are some lovely footpaths. The wood contains several rare species of plants and fungi and many are listed for special protection in a Yorkshire Wildlife Trust nature reserve.

I love the villages of Wharfedale, particularly Kettlewell, Appletreewick and Burnsall. Burnsall, on a loop in the river with attractive bridge and fell, must be one of the prettiest places in the country and the

This is one of my favourite views of the Wharfe, which is a truly lovely river. The photographer is standing at Kirk Bank, just down the road from Kilnsey, looking across towards Grass Wood and Conistone.

road past Appletreewick, or 'Aptrick' as it's known, provides another of my favourite views of the Wharfe. Before we got to know people at Kettlewell, my wife Veronica and I used to go to a pub at Appletreewick regularly and had a lot of fun with friends up there. We had some happy times – such as at Christmas and on New Year's Eve.

The trouble is when you get places so beautiful they can be spoiled a little by attracting too many people. But I do understand that visitors want to share these places. And all I ask is that they leave the dale as they found it. Leaving your rubbish and paper bags behind is disgraceful. By all means come and enjoy a picnic, but you've got to think about farmers and their animals and I really wish that some people would take a bigger interest in the countryside when they visit our beautiful Dales.

At one time, before legislation (which seems to ruin everyone's life) came in, you could stop off in the dale and buy delicious, home-made cheeses from the farms. And you could get a bed and breakfast for 15 shillings (75p) – with a proper farmhouse breakfast, too.

I love to tell people about Ilkley Golf Club, where I am a member. It's a most beautiful course which runs right beside the Wharfe. The first seven holes are played by the river and that's when you can see the different moods of the river. Some days the water roars and on others it is beautiful and calm. On the right-hand side where the river splits, you can see the water running down very fast and, on the other side, you can see beautiful trout in the water. The wildlife on the banks of the Wharfe there is unbelievable. I've seen a ring ouzel down there, sand martins, dippers, wild duck, Canada geese and kingfishers. It's fascinating to play golf beside the Wharfe.

Another lovely place on the Wharfe is Linton, where the river plunges over the rocks in powerfall falls. A footbridge gives visitors a grandstand view.

The area around the back road from Barden Tower to Appletreewick and the road past Appletreewick and up to Pateley Bridge is said to be the most evil part of Wharfedale. I've even heard of people in the past praying, on bended knee, against evil up in that area, though I don't know how true those stories are.

I was once filming at Trollers Gill for a local television company, doing a piece about Barguest, the legendary spectral hound supposed to live up there and said to have eyes as big as saucers. It was a most beautiful day and suddenly the blackest cloud you've ever seen appeared from nowhere, right above us, just as we were talking about Barguest on camera. There was thunder, lightning and rain, but the storm moved on in about 15 minutes. The way it happened was weird.

Just to walk over the tops of Wharfedale is absolutely incredible and something completely different. Apart from the presence of motor cars the valley is, as far as I'm concerned, just like it was years and years ago.

They used to film the television soap Emmerdale Farm in Arncliffe, giving the tiny village national fame. It has a group of attractive cottages grouped around a picturesque green. The telephone box in this picture must be one of the most-photographed in the country! Arncliffe was built on a gravel delta and is the only settlement in Littondale south of the river Skirfare.

Conistone is the sort of village invented for picture postcards. It has a charm and scale with great appeal. The village is tucked away on the 'quiet' side of Wharfedale, opposite the busy road which passes through Kilnsey on its way to Kettlewell. Conistone boasts a number of attractive cottages, many of which have glorious floral displays in season.

There are several stunning limestone features around and above the dry valley of Conistone Dib. Here's a view of a rather splendid crag up on the tops. The village of Conistone, which can trace its history back to Saxon times, lies opposite the famous Kilnsey Crag. This is a fascinating part of Wharfedale.

In England, the bird's eye primrose is found only in the Yorkshire Dales, the Durham Dales and parts of Cumbria. This example was photographed under Kilnsey Crag. About two inches high from ground to flower it grows in abundance in Wharfedale, where there are great carpets of it between May and early June.

The mountain pansy, a cheerful little flower which could almost be an emblem for the Dales. A lover of limestone terrain, it comes in a variety of colours, but in its pure yellow form is found only in the Dales.

There are several extensive areas of
limestone pavement in the Dales and
one fine example can be found above
Conistone Dib. Two rather scraggy
trees cling to a precarious existence in
this bleak landscape.

Left. The Wharfe may be a beautiful river, but it also has its dangerous parts. None more so than the rocky cleft of The Strid, near Bolton Abbey. Here, the water gushes down a channel just six feet wide at its narrowest point. This is certainly not the place to lose your footing as the river can be up to 25 feet deep. The Strid means 'stride', but you'd have to be pretty stupid to attempt the leap. I believe legend has it that a white horse appears when someone has drowned in The Strid.

Below. Yew Cogar Scar, on the right, and Cowside Beck are in a side gorge close to Arncliffe. As you can see from this picture, it's a wild and rugged place. Again, there is plenty of limestone visible, in sharp contrast to the green of the grass.

The river Skirfare is a tributary of the
Wharfe and flows down Littondale to
join the main valley near Kilnsey. The
parish church at Arncliffe is a much-
photographed subject and makes a fine
sight looking over the bridge through
leafless trees.

A view of the Wharfe upstream from
Kettlewell, oozing the atmosphere of
the Dales. Dry-stone walls and barns
add a pleasing touch to the rising slopes
of the valley side.

The historic village of Burnsall is one of my favourite places in Wharfedale. There's a beautiful sweep of the river and an attractive bridge. Unfortunately, everyone knows just how nice Burnsall is and it can get very busy in the summer months. The village has an annual Sports event each August and its fell race is one of the oldest around, dating from around 1850.

Climb up on to the tops above Wharfedale and, in winter, you'll often have only the sheep for company. This is a shot of Old Cote Moor, overlooking Littondale. This area of land separates the Wharfe and the Skirfare.

Glorious autumnal shades make for a
striking picture on Barden Moor, above
Wharfedale.

Pages 56, 57. In books from years ago,
writers would talk of the "fast flowing
Wharfe". Here, upstream from Barden
Bridge, the water is in lively mood on a
chilly, wintry day.

A wonderful shot of dry-stone walls at Cowside in Littondale. When the walls follow the curves of the land in this way, they definitely add something to what is already an attractive scene.

What a wonderful contrast in brilliant
colours in this view of a field barn and
ragwort at Skyreholme, just down the
road from Appletreewick. Barns are a
real feature of the Dales and make a
heartwarming sight. Not far from here is
Trollers Gill, famed as the lair of the
legendary spectral hound called
Barguest.

Wensleydale

Semer Water is a lovely, secluded spot a short distance from the main dale. The river Bain, at two miles in length said to be the shortest river in England, drains out of what is a glacial lake on its way to the charming village of Bainbridge. I believe the surface covers about 90 acres and there is water skiing here during the summer. By the lakeshore is the Carlow Stone, a great boulder dumped many, many years ago by the retreating ice.

Wensleydale isn't everyone's cup of tea. Some people say its floor is too wide to make it truly spectacular, while others feel it lacks the wildness and isolation of Swaledale. But there is so much of interest in the dale – and so many wonderful sights to enjoy.

My favourite spot is the famous Aysgarth Falls, where the river Ure plunges over a series of rock shelves in quite awesome fashion. The last time I was there, we'd had a lot of rain and, by God, was the water in spate. It was rushing through. The millions of gallons of water pouring over the falls was unbelievable. I must have been there half a dozen times and I've never seen the falls in such a state. The wheel on the old mill by the road bridge must have had a control on it. If not, like this, it would have taken the wheel off. It would have gone down the river and finished up in Leyburn!

Aysgarth has a National Park Centre which I had the great honour of opening in 1997. The buildings used to be workers' cottages. When I asked them why they wanted me, they said they wanted a famous Yorkshire person. I was flattered, really, that they asked me. They even had a plaque made, which I thought was a wonderful gesture. It's nice to take a break for a cup of tea and a bite to eat at the centre – the people there are wonderful and nothing is too much trouble for them to help you.

When my son-in-law came over from America I took him up to Aysgarth to show him the falls and the plaque in the centre's reception area and he was thrilled to bits with both. He just couldn't believe the Dales and was absolutely flabbergasted by the beauty of the countryside. He talked about the Dales for hours.

On the day of the opening ceremony, local craftsman Colin Simpson was working there. Colin produces hay rakes, pegs, mallets and brooms in the old fashioned way. I helped him out and it was absolutely marvellous to see him at work.

They have a fox in the centre's reception area. It has been preserved after being knocked down and killed in the road. It's not very big, but it's a beautiful thing.

There's a pub in Aysgarth called the George and Dragon. By all accounts, one former landlady was a bit of a dragon. They say people used to knock on the door and ask her if George was in!

One of the things everyone associates with Wensleydale is the crumbly white cheese which bears the dale's name. The creamery is at Hawes – and they make some delicious cheeses. There's a little shop in Aysgarth where the full range is on sale. On my last visit, I bought some Wensleydale with Old Peculiar, with stem ginger and some of the blue. They also sell some interesting wines. They have elderberry, dandelion and parsnip wines – that's fighting stuff, by God.

Wensleydale is, of course, known to millions as Herriot country. James Herriot, or to give him his real name Alf Wight, was a lovely man who wrote those wonderful books which were later made into films and a television series. I had the great pleasure of meeting Alf and he spoke with great affection for the Dales. He was, I suppose, like me, an offcumd'en, not born in the Dales. Although he had a Scottish accent, he was a Wearsider. He trained to become a vet and had a surgery in Thirsk, where they still talk about him with great affection.

At one of our meetings, we swopped books. I signed one for him and he signed one for me. He was a wonderful man and I believe they are going to build some sort of memorial centre for him at Thirsk, which would be very fitting. When we met, he used to chat – and he loved his cricket. He is missed in the Dales because, through his books, he sold the Dales to the whole world.

Mentioning cricket brings to mind a chance meeting I had with a former cricketer in West Witton, the village which lies under the slopes of Penhill. There's a well-known hostelry there called the Wensleydale Heifer and I was in there one night with eight or nine others after playing cricket at Sedbergh in Dentdale. We'd called in for ham and eggs and a couple of glasses of wine.

The landlord came up to me and said: "There's somebody in the hotel who'd like to meet you, Freddie." The chap came towards me and I said: "Hello. Your name's Arthur Carr." And it was. He was the old Nottinghamshire

Hardraw Force is a truly awe-inspiring sight when the water is bursting up and over the rocks, almost 100 feet above the pool at its foot. On my last visit, the falls were even more impressive than in this view and the natural amphitheatre echoed with sound and fury. Talking of sound, close by is the site of the hamlet's annual brass band contest.

Bolton Castle dominates the rising ground above the river Ure between Leyburn and Redmire. I believe the castle was really a large, fortified manor house and its conversion into the mini-fortress we see today didn't take place until the 14th century. The work, which cost £12,000, was completed on the instructions of Richard le Scrope, Chancellor to the King, Richard III.

A magnificent view of Bolton Castle, a most imposing place. This was one of the buildings in which Mary Queen of Scots was held on her journey from the vulnerable frontier castle at Carlisle to more secure prisons in the south of England in the 16th century. Her stay was six months long. She must have had plenty of time to contemplate the glorious views across the dale towards Penhill, though legend has it that she escaped, only to be recaptured at a spot now called Queen's Gap.

and England captain. I asked what someone from so far south was doing in Wensleydale. It turned out he'd moved up to West Witton and he told me how much he liked it.

We reminisced about playing the Australians and he talked about great cricketers such as Larwood, Voce, Bradman, Sutcliffe and Hobbs. It was absolutely wonderful to be in the middle of nowhere talking about some of the most famous cricketers in history. Old cricketers tend to reminisce like that when they get together – and they catch every catch, hit every half-volley for four and the only time they ever got out was when they weren't ready!

There's a lot of old folk stories about in Yorkshire – and Wensleydale isn't any different. One relating to West Witton is the Burning of Owd Bartle, which takes place late in August each year. Owd Bartle's tale is pure folklore, with scarcely a scrap of hard evidence to suggest it is a

true account. The story most often told is that Owd Bartle was a sheep-stealer who, having been caught in the act, was chased from the heights of Penhill to the edge of the village, where he met his end. The chase, which was started about 400 years ago as a warning to other light-fingered folk, is re-enacted annually and an effigy of the likeable rogue is then soaked in paraffin and ceremoniously burned.

Another spot in Wensleydale I love and adore is Hardraw Force, a spectacular fall of almost 100 feet. You approach the falls after paying a small charge in the Green Dragon Inn. When I was last there, we'd had a great deal of rain in the Dales and the water was thumping down. I couldn't get over the sound — it was like thunder. The power of the water was unbelievable. Walking back from the falls, I passed the site of the annual brass band contest. The bands must really sound great in that wonderful natural amphitheatre.

I like to look at the headstones in the graveyard of the tiny church in Hardraw. One stone dates back to 1829. How must people have lived up there all those years ago? They must have got about by horse and cart and been self-sufficient. On the subject of food, there's a cafe in Hardraw called the Shepherd's Kitchen — a lovely name. There's a nice sign outside which reads:

You're welcome to park for go see the fall,
But after you've been, please give us a call.

That means 'go spend a bob or two'.

Nearby is the lovely village of Bainbridge, which has a pub full of character called the Rose and Crown overlooking the green. I was up there once filming for a local television company doing a story about the famous horn they have in the pub. It was once used to summon foresters from their labours and is now blown during the evenings of Michaelmas and Shrovetide. I had a go, but couldn't get a sound out of it!

I heard quite recently of the work of the Wensleydale Railway Association. I understand its members want to re-open the line which runs down the dale from Northallerton all the way out to the Settle to Carlisle at Garsdale. I'm sure it would be a big tourist attraction and a lovely way to see the dale. People would come for miles to ride on the train. It seems a very ambitious scheme, but I certainly wish them well with it.

Semer Water is prone to flash flooding
and I was once told about a poem which
is thought to have its origins in an
ancient settlement being engulfed by
its waters. They were romantic words
about the lake, harking back to a
tradition of a proud city, cursed by a
beggar who had been refused food and
drink, and was flooded in dramatic
fashion.

There are many wonderful waterfalls in Wensleydale and one of the finest is Whitfield Gill Force, up above Askrigg. I've often stood at the edge of the pool below the falls and smoked a quiet pipe, but I've never had this remarkable view. The photographer must have been very sure-footed to go behind the tumbling waters!

Below. Winter's grip is icy and tight in the Dales. I'm almost shivering just to look at this view of a very cold day on the River Ure near Aysgarth. Wensleydale is the only main dale not to be named after the river which runs through it, though many years ago it bore the name Uredale or Yoredale, and I very occasionally still hear it.

Hawes is, I find, a bustling market town, but you don't have to venture far beyond its limits to find yourself plunged into the most tranquil of countryside. Snow adds another dimension to Wensleydale's beauty and this is a lovely morning shot of a winter's day close to Hawes.

FRED TRUEMAN'S DALES JOURNEY

When the snow lies thickly on the ground and a chill wind gusts down the length of the valley, Wensleydale can be an inhospitable place. At least these feeding sheep have their fleeces to keep them warm! This is a view close to West Burton, through which village flows the delightful Walden Beck.

Pages 72, 73 Middleham Castle, which dates from the 12th century, is another of Wensleydale's majestic structures. The later King Richard III, who died in the Battle of Bosworth in 1485, was raised in the castle and his only son, Edward, was born within its impressive walls. Middleham is also well known for its successful string of racing stables.

Haylands Bridge is a charming spot on the Brunt Acres Road between Hawes and Hardraw. Its clean, elegant lines are very pleasing to my eye. This place isn't far from the attractive Hawes cricket ground – in fact a lusty blow of the bat would probably send a ball far enough to land in the water.

Arthur Carr, the former Nottinghamshire and England cricket captain, made his home in West Witton – and this view shows why he liked the village so much. The photographer is standing on the slopes of Penhill, with the village in the middle ground. I met Arthur quite by chance in that well-known West Witton hostelry, the Wensleydale Heifer. We had a wonderful chat about some of the great players from cricket's rich history.

When Wensleydale's flat, wide, verdant floor is carpeted with daisies and buttercups, it makes a splendid sight. This view, with the rusty farm equipment in the foreground, also reminds me that the land here is very much a workplace for some. Wensleydale is good farming country.

Cotterdale is a short, secluded valley
leading off the main dale above Hawes.
Its beck runs into the Ure after passing
through some beautiful meadows.
There are very few homes in
Cotterdale, which boasts all the peace,
quiet and privacy a man could wish for.

Wonderful light illuminates the River Ure and the red roofs and buff walls of West Tanfield, which is well downstream and close to Ripon. The picturesque village's famous 15th century Marmion Tower is on the extreme left of this view. It is a gatehouse of a long-vanished ancestral home. Sir Walter Scott based his novel *Marmion* on the family, but there is no record of anyone of that name being at the Battle of Flodden.

Wensleydale has many wonderful buildings – and one of them is Jervaulx Abbey. It was a Cistercian abbey founded in 1156 after the monks decided it was a rather less bleak spot than the one they had been inhabiting higher up the valley. Sadly, there isn't that much left to see because a lot of the stones have, over the centuries, been used to patch up other buildings in the district.

The slopes of Addlebrough loom over the tiny settlement of Worton, opposite Askrigg on the south bank of the River Ure. It's a peaceful spot, with well-tended buildings and, as this view shows, immaculate fences.

Swaledale

Changing moods and colours are a familiar aspect of the Dales. This is haymaking time near Thwaite. Just look at all those barns dotted around!

When I recall outings to Swaledale, the most northerly of the Yorkshire Dales, I always thinks of its barns. Everywhere you look in the valley, you can see barns, big and small. There's a spot near Gunnerside where you can stand alongside the road and from that vantage point, you can count about 30 barns.

I wonder why there are so many in such close proximity and in such obscure places. It intrigues me. There must be a reason. The farmers probably used them for storing animal feed to save them carrying it out across the fields and up the slopes. I bet they even sheltered their animals in the barns over the winter.

I was pleased to hear of the scheme to provide Heritage Lottery Fund grants to pay for restoring these wonderful barns. Many of them are in a poor state of repair. Farmers today simply don't have the time or money to spend on restoring the barns, many of which don't have much use now. Though a huge task, it's a marvellous idea that this sort of heritage and tradition should be kept alive.

Swaledale is a beautiful dale – and the barns seem to break it up more than the other dales. There's a lot to be seen in the valley and a lot of history in it, too. In contrast to Wensleydale, it is much narrower and also, particularly up around Thwaite and Keld, more rugged. The dale has, like the other dales, a character all of its own and looking down the valley from Keld, you can see for miles. It has its own beauty, of that there is no doubt, with the contours of the land set off by hundreds of miles of dry-stone walls. The walls here really are magnificent. I look at them and can only imagine how much work went into building them. Swaledale is one of those dales where you should book in somewhere for two or three nights to give yourself a chance to really explore the place.

Swaledale is, of course, very famous for its hill sheep, with the black nose. People do say they are a very hardy breed and looking at the terrain, they would have to be. When the sun is shining early in the summer, it's lovely to watch the lambs springing around.

When I go up to Keld, I think: "What do the people do up here?" It's so remote. A few houses in the middle of nowhere. All I can say is that if a foreign power ever invaded this country, Keld is the place I'd go because I don't think they'd ever find it! In its own way, it's absolutely beautiful. You've got the scenery and the fresh air, the tranquillity and the peace of mind. Marvellous.

But you have to be a special kind of person to live somewhere like Keld. There's nothing there. No amenities or anything. The hamlet has some lovely little cottages and barn conversions, though – just the sort of thing I'd love if I lived in Leeds or Bradford.

Waterfalls are a feature of the top end of the Swale – and Keld seems to be surrounded by them. There are a couple of crackers I love to see after heavy rain. Kisdon Force and Wainwath Force are worth a moment of anyone's time. I believe the name Keld means 'spring' – it's very appropriate.

One thing I have noticed in some of the houses in Swaledale is the habit of putting plastic bags in the outside corners of the windows. It's to stop house martins and swallows building their nests. It's a shame because the birds in the valley are so friendly. I remember once stopping for a pint in Thwaite, at the Kearton Guest House. It was lovely, sitting there in the afternoon sun, enjoying my pipe. A sparrow, a tame little fella, hopped along the wall to say hello. I bet people throw crumbs to them – and they know that. This sparrow was so tame it almost seemed to want to perch on my outstretched hand. He came down, touched my hand and then flew off.

Kearton is an honoured surname in Swaledale. Richard Kearton was born in Thwaite and went on to be a pioneer of wildlife photography. A cottage in the village, which is hemmed in by the hills of Great Shunner Fell, Kisdon and Lovely Seat, has a stone surround on its front door carved with the initials of Richard and his brother, Cherry. It also has carvings of birds and beasts and is a splendid reminder of the two.

Although Swaledale today is a quiet place, not too long ago it was a busy centre for lead mining. The scars of mining can still be seen up

Gunnerside Gill, in Arkengarthdale and around Surrender Bridge. There are the remains of the old smelt mills and many piles of spoil. It's hard to believe that where now there is such a peace and beauty once there was the noise and bustle of industry. I always feel this is an eerie part of Swaledale, as if it's haunted by memories.

Now the miners have gone, Gunnerside Gill is a great place for wild flowers. One in particular to look out for is the spring sandwort, which has a distinctive star-shaped flower, and is somehow able to thrive in the lead-laden soil.

In many ways, Richmond is the gateway to Swaledale. It's a wonderfully atmospheric town, steeped in history and legend. The striking keep of its sandstone castle, perched on a cliff high above the river, dominates the surrounding country and its narrow streets and large cobbled square tell of a colourful past. There's a legend which says that in England's hour of need, King Arthur and his Knights of the Round Table will emerge from a cavern under the castle. I'm told Richmond has been described as one of 35 most precious towns in England – and I can only agree with that sentiment.

Coming down the dale from Richmond on the main road, watch out for a sharp right-hand turn which leads to Marske. It's a quiet village, set back from the main valley in the shadow of wooded hills and has a secretive sort of atmosphere. This lush setting rivals Burnsall, in Wharfedale, for sheer beauty. While there, you'll probably spot one or two hikers doing the Coast to Coast Walk, which marches the length of Swaledale.

The area around Reeth, sheltering beneath Fremington Edge, is lovely. The large green is a useful place to stop and there are a couple of nice pubs serving good beer. Here, you can turn off to go down Arkengarthdale, which is even more peaceful than Swaledale. The river bridge over the Arkle Beck at Langthwaite featured in All Creatures Great and Small, the televised versions of James Herriot's marvellous stories of a Dales vet. Just up the hill from Langthwaite is a collection of cottages with the wonderful name of Booze. That one always makes me smile, because despite the name, there's no pub!

A favourite drive of mine in the Dales is up and over the Buttertubs Pass, which links Swaledale with Wensleydale. You can turn off between

Muker and Thwaite and climb steeply up to the mass of land called Abbotside Common which separates the two valleys. I love and adore it up there – it feels like you're on top of the world. And it feels like you've got all the time in the world. The sheep up there certainly seem to think so as they plod lazily along the road, refusing to move over until the very last second.

The pass's intriguing name comes, apparently, from its cluster of limestone shafts, each of which has a depth of about 65 feet. Eventually, and reluctantly, the road drops down into Hardraw and on to the busy little market town of Hawes.

And there, reluctantly, I take my leave of Swaledale – a valley of peace, beauty and history.

Low cloud makes for a dramatic scene between Muker and Keld.

Meadows, barns and walls near Muker. The peace around here is shattered each September when the Muker Show is held. The fun begins with a procession to the show field, with the famous Muker Brass Band leading the way.

Pages 88, 89. As well as its barns, Swaledale is also noted for its wonderful meadows, which are a riot of colour at the right time of year. This one is at Usha Gap, near Muker.

A delightful picture of upper Swaledale near Keld. At this time of the year, the valley is wonderfully lush and green, with the folds of the land a delight to the eye.

The warm shades of the stone in Swaledale's village are seen at their best in mellow light. Here, the tower of Muker's church peers down upon some lovely old cottages.

Below. The classic view of Thwaite village, with its cottages clustered together next to the bridge. Its name comes from a Norse word meaning 'a clearing' in woodland.

FRED TRUEMAN'S DALES JOURNEY

Winter is starting to fade in this view of Muker, one of Swaledale's many charming villages. It's always nice to enjoy a drink outside the Farmers' Arms on a sunny afternoon, watching the village's life go by. The stream is Muker Beck, not the Swale, as many mistakenly think.

Left. Barns and meadows, looking at their springtime best, in upper Swaledale.

Right. The barns of Swaledale intrigue me. There are so many, in such close proximity, and often in such obscure places. Wherever you look in the valley, you can see a handful of barns. This view is at the top end of the dale.

Below. A farmer busily cuts hay at Usha Gap Farm, near Muker, as another works in the valley floor below.

The gruelling Pennine Way, all 268 miles of it, must be a wonderful walk and takes in some of the finest parts of the Dales. Here, there's no excuse for hikers taking the wrong turn near Thwaite.

A real slice of Swaledale here, with dry-stone walls and field barns contrasting with the steep, green sides of the valley. We are near Thwaite.

The highest pub in England – the Tan
Hill Inn. It stands at almost 1,800 feet
and is surrounded by moorland and the
cries of the lapwing, curlew and golden
plover.

Left. The area around Keld is well-known for its spectacular waterfalls. This is Kisdon Force, which drops through 30 feet and over several rock ledges in a deep limestone gorge. It's a wonderful spot.

Swaledale twists and turns in graceful fashion at its upper end. The road to Thwaite and Keld is visible in this view looking updale from above Muker. There's such a contrast with neighbouring Wensleydale here, with Swaledale much narrower and far more remote and rugged.

Impossibly brilliant colours near Reeth as a deep blue sky contrasts with the whiteness of the snow lying thickly on the ground.

The rugged nature of the top end of Swaledale is clear in this wintry view of Stonesdale Moor, in the hilly country beyond Keld. Even in this wilderness, dry-stone walls and barns have been built.

The arrival of winter brings a stark beauty to Swaledale. In this view, the flat valley floor sweeps away with the distant hills providing a pleasing backdrop.

Ribblesdale

Another of my favourite views of Penyghent, with the mountain looming menacingly over Dale Head Farm. This peaceful spot is just off the Silverdale road.

When I think of Ribblesdale, I think of four things: Penyghent, Ingleborough, Whernside and Ribblehead Viaduct, on the Settle to Carlisle Railway. You can see them all at Ribblehead from a wonderful vantage point just 20 feet off the road. What a beautiful sight they make!

One of the best ways to see Ribblesdale is on the railway. I've journeyed up through the dale that way many times and I remember one day I was sitting on the train, talking to two Americans and their wives. The men had been in the American air force during the war, had told their wives how beautiful the Dales were and had promised, one day, to bring them over. This is exactly what they had done. They'd come all the way from America and were making a special effort to take their respective ladies up over the Dales on this beautiful railway. I always wish I could have met the four of them again to hear what they thought of the Dales. I guarantee that they would have said it was a beautiful part of the world.

These days on the railway we have to ride around in carriages like cattle trucks with an engine back and front, but really someone ought to put together a package to have steam engines running regularly up there. When we do have a steam engine on the line, it's a wonderful attraction. There are people everywhere, on the bridges and the embankments, with their cameras. To me, the railway is the most scenic route in Britain. It's marvellous to see all that beautiful countryside as you pull up over the tops.

Ribblehead Viaduct is, to my mind, a piece of history not repeated anywhere else in Britain. It's a part of our national heritage and shouldn't be allowed to crumble away. Its twenty-four limestone arches are a magnificent feat of engineering and should stand for all time. Although I've ridden over the viaduct on the train many times, I've never seen a train crossing the viaduct. It must be a wonderful sight to watch a steam train, with those lovely old Pullman carriages, going over it in the middle of nowhere. I'd love to see that.

It's so beautiful up there, at all times of the year. There's a special grandeur in the winter, with the snow capping each of the Three Peaks. It's like a miniature Switzerland. But it's very wild up at Ribblehead. I can't imagine what it must have been like for the navvies building the railway, living with their families in shanty towns. If the living conditions were bad, the working conditions must have been at least as tough – in baking sun one minute and then up to their arms in water the next.

The last time I was up in Ribblesdale, I stopped in Horton to visit the Penyghent Cafe, which is the starting and finishing point for the famous Three Peaks Walk. I asked for a cup of coffee and got about a pint and a half – I've never seen a mug so big. While there, I saw the famous clock and found out what it is all about. If you do the Three Peaks challenge, which covers about 25 miles and some 5,000 feet of climbing, in less than 12 hours, you qualify for membership of the Three Peaks of Yorkshire Club. It's a real test and those who run it in two-and-a-half hours must be as fit as a butcher's dog! To make sure no-one cheats, like the old factory days, you clock in when you start and when you come back, clock out. It's wonderful that something like this exists.

While I was sitting there I saw a piece of Yorkshire I couldn't believe. I bought a postcard which featured a farmer's sign reading: 'Tek care, lambs on't road.' It was one of the funniest I've ever seen and I couldn't resist it. Anyone from outside Yorkshire seeing that would think it was in a foreign language! I'm going to frame one and send the other to my son-in-law, who was a Dales farmer and now lives abroad. It'll make him smile.

Just outside the cafe, there is a magical view of Penyghent, visible between the trees on the far side of the road. It takes me back to South Africa and standing on the cricket ground at Newlands. There, you look across and there is Table Mountain and, I think, Lion Mountain, so named because of its likeness to the shape of a lion. Penyghent is very similar and reminds me of that similar view in South Africa all those thousands of miles away. The resemblance between the two mountains is uncanny.

Pages 104, 105. Stainforth Bridge is a lovely old structure, spanning the Ribble with a graceful sweep. It dates from the 17th century and is a great spot from which to watch the water bubbling below on its way to the falls lower down the river. I believe the bridge was provided by the Quaker owner of nearby Knight Stainforth Hall.

Now here's a sight I'd love to see – a train rumbling across the Ribblehead Viaduct. It's not a steam engine, but then you can't have everything. The Settle to Carlisle line is, to my mind, the best way to see Ribblesdale. Though I've crossed the viaduct many times on board trains, whenever I've been standing on the ground beneath its 24 arches, I've never been lucky enough to catch one going over.

That's a nice thing about the Three Peaks – each has its own distinctive outline. If Penyghent is like a lion, Whernside must be a whale. I'm not sure about Ingleborough – but the view looking back to it from the road over to Hawes is wonderful.

One thing I don't approve of around Horton and neighbouring Helwith Bridge is the quarrying. Horton, in particular, is a lovely village and it's such a shame that the skyline around has been scarred by industry. I don't feel that quarrying should be allowed to take place in a National Park.

It's always nice to approach Ribblesdale from the Settle direction. Settle is a bustling little town where I've played cricket many times. There's a salmon leap along the river there, too, and people like to go and watch the fish. The Ribble separates the town from the neighbouring village of Giggleswick, which is famous for its public school. Once you turn off the main road and head up towards Langcliffe and Stainforth, it's like you've entered another world. You really feel that after the roar of the A65 you're firmly back in the Dales.

The falls at Stainforth are one of my favourite places in Ribblesdale. It's lovely to stand on the graceful single arch of the 17th century packhorse bridge and watch the peaty-brown waters of the river pass by underneath before they pick up speed and tumble over the rocks just a little way lower down. Nearby, is another well-known waterfall, Catrigg Force, which is well worth the steep pull up from the valley floor.

Driving up to Ribblehead, the country becomes bleaker and bleaker. When I pass the old Midland Railway cottages at the wonderfully-named Salt Lake, I try and think what it must be like living out here. It's so wild. There aren't any shops and the nearest doctor must be miles away.

Selside is a pleasant little hamlet and there's a nice touch with one of the buildings bearing the nameboard which was once on the old railway signalbox. The last time I was up there, there was a wonderful dappling of light and shade on the fields going up to Ribblehead. At Selside, there's a house where you pay a small sum to follow a lane and path to Alum Pot, one of many vast potholes in the limestone in Ribblesdale.

Once at Ribblehead, I'm often amused by the sheep and their lambs.

Here's an inviting stile on a footpath in the shadow of Ingleborough's menacing slopes. I'm full of admiration for anyone who attempts the Three Peaks Walk, on which Whernside, Ingleborough and Penyghent have to be climbed in less than 12 hours. Start and finish point is the Penyghent Cafe in Horton. This houses that wonderful clock which ensures no-one cheats – all walkers are required to fill in a registration card and clock out and clock in. Their departure time is stamped on the card, which also carries details of their home phone number, or that of where they are staying, car registration number and where it is parked. Those completing the challenge inside the time allowed are able to buy a certificate and a badge.

They walk slowly and carefully along the road, oblivious to the traffic. Where else could you see that?

It amazes me up there, in the shadow of the viaduct, that you get so many little streams which in such a short distance become a raging river. And as the river widens, the bird life increases. There are wonderful birds, such as dippers and kingfishers, to be seen lower down.

The Ribble is a strange river. In many ways, I associate it with Lancashire as it heads west down its valley through Blackburn and out into the Irish Sea beyond Preston. It may not spend too much of its life in Yorkshire, but while it does, the country around is absolutely marvellous.

Jack Frost coats the fields around Stockdale Farm, up above Settle. Attermire Scar looms in the background. Stockdale Beck is the watercourse in the bottom of the picture.

FRED TRUEMAN'S DALES JOURNEY

Lonely farms are dotted around the
wild and bleak landscape in Three
Peaks country. It must be a tough place
to live during the summer months, but
in winter conditions like these, with
Rainscar Farm nestling beneath the
slopes of Penyghent, I can't imagine
what life must be like.

I love and adore the wonderfully
peaceful country above the village of
Stainforth. This is a pleasant wintry
scene at Winskill. There's not a soul
about. Marvellous. From Stainforth,
you can follow an old packhorse road
over Penyghent Fell to Halton Gill at
the head of Littondale.

Ingleborough is a commanding spectacle from many places in the Dales. This dramatic shot is taken in Widdale, with the mountain appearing almost like a ship rising out of a heavy sea.

Below. I always think Ingleborough's shape is unmistakable – from whichever vantage point the mountain is viewed. This is the way its profile appears from Green Edge, looking across a section of limestone pavement.

Dales-bred sheep add interest to a
dramatic view high on the tops above
Ribblesdale.

I marvel at the patience and planning
that must go into securing a picture
like this. This is Ingleborough, seen
from Widdale, in silhouette against a
moody sky.

It's early morning on the slopes of Ingleborough and the photographer has only sheep for company. The second highest of the Three Peaks has a highly distinctive outline, instantly recognisable from wherever in the Dales it is spotted.

In cloudy weather, Ingleborough's
mood changes as the mountain presents
a more sombre face to the watching
world. The dark skyline around the
peak in this picture contrasts sharply
with the limestone cliffs of Moughton
Scars.

Right. Chapel-le-Dale is a short distance from Ribblesdale, but its squat little church, St Leonard's, has strong links with the valley. For in its graveyard is a poignant memorial to those who died building the magnificent Settle to Carlisle railway. More than 200 are buried here in unmarked graves. Most died when smallpox swept through the pitiful trackside shanty towns in which they lived.

Below. This really is one of the classic shots of Ribblesdale. We're looking at St Oswald's Church in Horton village, with the 'crouching lion' of Penyghent providing a distinctive and magnificent backdrop. Penyghent, the lowest of the Three Peaks, takes me back to my days of playing cricket at Newlands, in South Africa. The ground there was overlooked by a mountain which bore an uncanny resemblance to Penyghent.

The popularity of the Three Peaks with walkers has led to a great deal of footpath erosion. This is an example on the summit of Penyghent. A great deal of work has been done to repair such damage. Note Ingleborough in the background, peering over the scene.

There is some stunning limestone scenery in the hills above Settle and Langcliffe. Attermire Scar is a particularly interesting place. It is pockmarked with shake holes and caves as water has its inevitable erosive effect on the limestone landscape. There are two large caves to be seen here – named Attermire and Horseshoe.

The natural and man-made worlds collide in limestone in this view of Attermire Scar. Dry-stone walls are a trademark feature of the Dales. The work that goes into building them and then ensuring they withstand the worst the Pennine weather can hurl at them really is astounding. Such walls are part of the heritage of the Dales and every effort must be made to ensure their survival.

Pages 120, 121. Here's another view of Stainforth Bridge, looking towards it from the falls. I love and adore the many falls in the Dales and the Ribble at this point provides a spectacular sight, especially after a few days of heavy rain.

Airedale and Malhamdale

A lovely scene taken from the road between Malham and Arncliffe. The sheep have been safely gathered in and the light is fading on another farming day.

I regard the treasures of the Malham area as heaven-sent. You couldn't buy them – they're put there by the Lord above. One of the becks which later joins with another to form the River Aire rises out of Malham Tarn, disappears into the limestone and re-emerges beyond Malham Cove. Another appears at the foot of the Cove's sheer limestone cliffs before winding down through the village. If that's not enough, a short walk away are the wonders of Gordale Scar and Janet's Foss.

Although Wharfedale is my favourite dale, it doesn't have anything that compares with the Cove, which it seems time has passed by. It's something to behold and a piece of God's beauty. I'm so lucky to live so close to the Cove. It's just 15 minutes' drive from my home. Other people have to travel miles to see it and yet it's on my doorstep.

When I stand right under the sheer walls of the Cove on the banks of the river, I think what an unbelievably stunning place it is. Some people may think it looks stark, but to me it is a glorious spot. I believe that many years ago, the waters flowed over the lip of the Cove in a massive waterfall. It must have been a most spectacular sight.

People from the south of England have no idea of the outstanding beauty of places like Malham Cove. They seem to think Yorkshire is all about chimney stacks and smoke. I don't really want millions of people coming up here, but the Cove is part of our natural heritage and they can't be blamed for wanting to see it.

No matter when I go to the Cove, whether the sun is shining or its face is dull, there's a feeling of tranquillity about it. It's difficult to explain, but with its different moods, it seems to be like a person. Whatever the weather, a character still seems to come out of it. What could be nicer than sitting under the Cove, smoking a pipe, with a flask of coffee and a sandwich on a sunny day. It's paradise, absolute paradise. Really,

I could write four or five thousand words on the Cove alone.

It's funny how the surroundings up at the Cove rub off on those who visit it. People walk along the path from the road and wish each other a good morning. I reckon it's because they are enjoying themselves.

The last time I went up to Gordale Scar I was lucky to go on a day after we'd had several days of heavy rain. The amount of water powering through the Scar was unbelievable. To see the falls pouring down through the very top rocks was a first for me.

The falls are majestic. They are superb. To stand among the rocks at the foot of the falls and hear the water echoing around that amphitheatre is an awe-inspiring experience.

This is another place in the Dales where you get the feeling the landscape has always been the same. It's untouched, unspoiled and that's the way I hope it's always going to be.

Walking back down the path from the Scar, I was amazed to see water springing up just about everywhere. It would bubble out of the ground and then within 30 or 40 yards be flowing along at a hell of a pace. Looking at the amount of water around, we should never have a water shortage in the Dales!

I stood alongside Gordale Beck and it smelled beautiful. I thought I could hear a radio from one of the cars parked nearby, but it was the sound of water running over a rock. It was amazing, like the water was talking to me. And just a bit further downstream, the water was making an entirely different sound.

One of the lovely things about Gordale Scar is that you don't see the falls until the very last minute. They are hidden away round a corner. You can hear them, but you can't see them. Looking up to the Scar from the grass near the road where people camp, you'd never know the falls were there.

I then walked down to have a look at Janet's Foss, another spectacular cascade. It's a lovely spot to get a table out, have a few sandwiches and enjoy its beauty.

I believe the pool below the falls was, years ago, used as a sheepwash by the local farmers. They would wash the sheep in late June before shearing as they could get a better price for a cleaner fleece. The farmers would drive the sheep into the pool and then wash them, standing up to their waists in the water.

One of the wonders of the Malham area. This is Gordale Beck and Gordale Scar, an awe-inspiring place to visit when the rains have been falling. When walking up the path to the Scar from the road, you don't see the waterfall until the last moment – but you can hear it echoing around the natural amphitheatre. On my last visit, the water was gushing out of the very top of the Scar and was a magnificent sight. William Wordsworth visited the area in 1807 and described Gordale as "like a lair where young lions crouch".

Anyone climbing up from the Cove to visit Malham Tarn will pass through the dry valley of Watlowes. It's a fascinating place, full of shattered limestone and towering cliffs.

You can see dippers and grey wagtails alongside the water. What a painting this scene would make! I can just imagine Ashley Jackson sitting there painting Janet's Foss. And what a lovely place it would be to set up a band and have a 'Songs of Praise'. It would be packed with people.

High above Malham, the limestone seems to go on for miles, washed clean by the rains of time. Sometimes, I take it for granted that all this is on my doorstep, but then I go out for a walk around Malham and am brought back to earth by the glories of the scenery.

My dogs love the open spaces on the walk to Malham Tarn. Cassie is a cross-bred collie and Tessa a pure white samoyed, from Russia. Cassie got her name because I got her from a dogs' home in Castleford, which is, incidentally, on the Aire. I love my dogs – they are so loyal and friendly.

Gazing across the Tarn you can see Tarn House, which I always think is such an imposing place. And what a view! I can imagine what it must have been like when horse-drawn carriages were rolling up to the house. It must have been a lonely place to live, but what a tranquil place, in the middle of nowhere. So much peace and quiet. The only thing you'd hear would be the curlew calling or the lowing of cattle.

Malham is a lovely village and I used to go there often to eat at the Lister's Arms. An Italian, Pete I think his name was, used to do the most marvellous steaks and wonderful Italian wine. With Veronica, I used to sit by the lovely inglenook fireplace. Pete's steaks were a speciality, they were famous and he built a name for himself. We used to have great fun up there.

People say that if you see snow on the hills above Malham in November, we are in for a mild winter. It reminds me of the wonderful old country sayings about the weather we have in Yorkshire. It's amazing how true they are. One I've heard is:

If ice in November will bear a duck,
The rest of the winter is slush and muck.

Further down the river is Kirkby Malham, another attractive village. Willie Rushton, a very nice man, God bless his soul, once came up to the Dales and stayed with his good lady at the Victoria in Kirkby Malham. They came to our house, looked round the Dales and they thought it was all absolutely marvellous. They were introduced to Arnold the gravedigger, who was an odd job sort of a lad. He dug graves, did dry-stone walls and was a real character. Unfortunately, he died very suddenly, but they always reckon (and I don't know how true this is) that he got the sack because one day he was opening a grave to bury one relative next to another and dug a skull up.

As you go down the dale, following the Aire, there are more charming villages: Airton, Bell Busk and Gargrave, where I like to go and stand by the river and watch the trout. There are some big ones, too.

The upper Aire is absolutely stunning and doesn't really start getting messy until it reaches Keighley, where industry tends to take over. But even here the river was of great use, driving the wheels of the textile mills.

You'd never know there was such beauty at Malham if you didn't go and see it. And although it's not far from my home, I could live at Malham. At certain times of the year, it's quiet, right up my street. I could sit there on a summer evening, by the river as it runs through the centre of the village, and enjoy a pipe and a beer. Lovely.

It can get pretty bleak on the hills above Malham after heavy snowfall. This is Capon Hall Farm, an isolated spot, shivering beneath a blanket of the white stuff.

There are some charming stretches of
the Aire between Keighley and Skipton
– and none more lovely than this
section close to the charming village of
Kildwick. Once into Keighley and
beyond, the river is overtaken by
industry and loses much of its appeal.

Does Airedale lie at the end of the rainbow? The photographer was lucky enough to catch this charming scene at Tomlin Pastures, Silsden, near Keighley.

FRED TRUEMAN'S DALES JOURNEY

Tranquillity to enjoy in this view of a
plantation and grazing sheep on Eshton
Moor.

Bradley Moor, high above Airedale, is a riot of purple when the heather blooms late in the summer. The villages in the background are Glusburn and Cross Hills.

The hillside above Riddlesden, a suburb of Keighley, can be very colourful and a joy to behold at the right time of the year. This is part of Spring Crag Woods – a popular place for walkers.

Although Malham is packed with wondrous limestone features, the area south of the village has some pleasing, rolling countryside. This shot shows a delightful hay meadow, full of colour.

FRED TRUEMAN'S DALES JOURNEY

Gargrave is a beautiful spot nestling along the banks of the Aire and the countryside around the village is peaceful. Here, in early spring, a ewe tends to her lambs.

Pages 136, 137. Eshton, with grazing sheep, on a warm summer evening. Anyone driving in this area can't help but notice the Wilson family mansion, now a nursing home, which appears across a tract of parkland.

AIREDALE AND MALHAMDALE

Left. Snow descends on a quiet lane near Bradley, but doesn't seem to deter this dog and its owner taking a peaceful stroll.

Right. Deep, crisp and, well, almost even. Perhaps the postman has disturbed the snow in this stark view of Farnhill Hall.

Left. Winter's chill bites at Bradley. This is a very typical Dales scene, with the sheep feeding and the dry-stone walls following the contours up to the hilltop. Lovely.

Below. There's a definite chill in the air in this atmospheric view of a winter's sunset on the Aire. This scene is close to the attractive village of Cononley, between Keighley and Skipton.

AIREDALE AND MALHAMDALE

Sunset over the Aire near Skipton, with
the distant hills peering down on a still,
silent scene.

FRED TRUEMAN'S DALES JOURNEY

There's much farming activity in the wide valley floor of the Aire between Skipton and Keighley. Here, hay bales are loaded onto a trailer at Bradley, a lovely little village tucked away off the main road.